CAMI'S WRITING ADVENTURE

An Indie Author's Path to Success

CAMI CHECKETTS

Birch River
PUBLISHING

COPYRIGHT

Cami's Writing Adventure: An Indie Author's Path to Success

Copyright © 2022 by Cami Checketts

All rights reserved.

No part of this book may be reproduced in any form or by any electronic or mechanical means, including information storage and retrieval systems, without written permission from the author, except for the use of brief quotations in a book review.

DEDICATION

My mom—my biggest cheerleader.
My daddy—who thought I was "the greatest thing since sliced bread."
My husband—who supported me when most spouses would've given up.
My boys and daughter-in-law—who give me all kinds of funny lines,
hugs, and inspiration. Plus, they let me buy them stuff.

ENDORSEMENTS

"For years I've wondered how Cami does it. She accomplishes more in a month than I do in a year! Finally, we have a peek into her mind and her habits. Writing Adventure inspired me to be a better writer and a better person. Insightful and inspirational!"
Daniel Coleman, author of Jabberwocky and Hatter

"Cami is a bundle of fire, energy, and brilliance. I admire her dauntless work ethic and how she radiates optimism and goodness. It was a treat to get a peek into the innerworkings of her mind and how she approaches writing and life. Cami is an inspiration to me, both as a dear friend and a fellow author. I'm so grateful that Cami has the fearless drive to keep crafting those wonderful adventure stories of her heart! She will continue to lift and inspire me, along with countless others. The world is a much better place thanks to Cami and her beautiful take on love and life."
Jennifer Youngblood, USA Today Bestselling Author

"This book is Amazing! I don't think it just pertains to a writer either! It's amazing to read and take advice on the inner struggles, strengths, successes, and what works for one person may not work for another. Being positive, finding a positive support group. We all have that friend or friends that lift us up, and how to lift others up. What an awesome way to take us on a journey that helps give us insight on how to better ourselves and whatever we are doing! Love the quotes through the book and examples on a positive outlook. Love the advice in trusting God and the talents He has blessed us with! Great read with sound advice!"

Wendy Voitl, Reviewer

INTRODUCTION

I've put off writing a book on my experiences, tips, and path to success because like most authors I'm a bit of a hermit and I don't like to talk about myself. I would rather brag about my children, or write a story about one of the hundreds of friends in my head clamoring for their stories to be told. Plus, my boys, daughter-in-law, and the people in my head are a lot more charming, witty, and good-looking than I'll ever be.

Don't worry though, this book is ultra-short and soon I'll be back telling my imaginary friends' stories.

This is a random compilation of my background, the reasons I feel I've had success, some of my theories about writing and life, and any tips or secrets I hope could help other writers, or anyone wanting to succeed at their business or career.

I value love and kindness. A lot. That being said, some things I say in this book are blunt. If that offends anyone, I am terribly sorry.

If you want to know what I have done to be successful as a

writer, mother, wife, and follower of the Savior, the truth of what I've experienced and the winding path I took is all I can share.

I pray that what I say will lift and inspire. I hope to share these thoughts, experiences, and tips out of love and humility. Please take what helps and inspires you and use it. If anything I say or recommend doesn't help you, disregard it.

If I've learned anything in life, and my writing journey, it's that we all have our own path. As long as we walk that path with the Savior and with faith, working hard and trying to love and lift others, it'll be the right path for us.

Hugs and blessings to you,
Cami

Chapter One

HOW IT ALL BEGAN

Be one-hundred percent present in whatever you're doing.

The two questions I get asked most often are: "Did you always know you wanted to be a writer?" or "How did you get started writing?"

The answer to the first question is no. I never imagined I could be a writer.

I grew up on a dairy farm near a small town in Idaho. There were a hundred and twenty-one people in the town and we repainted the sign if someone died or a baby was born. No joke.

My parents both had college degrees from a large university, our house was filled with books, and it was expected that we all would work hard and be successful in school and life, but I didn't have grand dreams or illusions.

I had a lot of daydreams, read so voraciously I was reading the unabridged version of Les Misérables at twelve, and I constantly made up stories in my head, but authors were like superheroes to me. If someone would've told me I'd be an author someday, I would've said, "Sweet, and then I'll move into the space station I helped design on Mars." It just wasn't a vision I'd ever had.

Fast forward a lot of years. I was twenty-nine, and I'd graduated from Utah State University with a Bachelor's in Exercise Science. I'd married my incredible husband and was working part time as an aerobics instructor and personal trainer, but my primary focus was raising my two boys while my husband worked eighty hours a week building his business.

My second son was almost nine months old. Both of my boys were absolutely beautiful, fun, happy, and perfect ... and I was a hot mess. Looking back, we think it was those dang female hormones being out of whack from a combination of intensive fertility treatments, a miscarriage, and simply being a young, inexperienced mom with a spouse who was gone a lot.

I went to see my doctor and rattled off a weird list of unrelated symptoms. He immediately diagnosed postpartum depression. I thought he was off his rocker. I was a tough farm girl. We don't get depression. We work our butts off and if we get tired, we work harder, and we do it with a smile on our faces.

I told him thank you very much for wasting my time and my hundred dollars for the visit (doctors' visits were cheaper back then, and I didn't actually say that to my doctor, just thought it. I'm great at one-liners in my head).

So I went home and tried harder to be happy, smile, serve others, and exercise more. Truthfully, I was down in the dumps. Any time my boys were asleep, I slept too. I hated the way I was. My husband and I had prayed and yearned and undergone a lot of expensive treatments for babies. Now I had two perfect boys and I wasn't enjoying them like I wanted to. I knew I could break through this funk, but I didn't quite know how.

One day, my mom came to visit me, yanked me out of bed as only a loving mama can do, and told me, "Go downstairs and ... write me a book."

I remember looking at her strangely and thinking, "Write you a book?"

But like any obedient, half-asleep daughter, I walked downstairs, sat down at the computer, and started tapping out one of the many half-cocked stories in my head. Neither of us has any idea what inspired her to say that.

It turns out that creating something was what I needed. Who knew? I was grateful, busy, fulfilled, excited about my boys, my husband, my life, and my faith again. I was able to overcome the postpartum with something positive, and thankfully I haven't dealt with depression again.

I know that is not always the case and have great empathy for those who deal with depression or other emotional disorders. I pray for those who do and hope they'll find the right treatment and support.

It has been almost twenty years since that fateful day. Writing has been a rollercoaster of setbacks, dreams, and many hours of hard work. Writing has also given me a lot of confidence, joy, ability to share my stories, some of the most wonderful friends in this world, the chance to share my testimony and faith through fiction, and financial success.

I haven't had time for a nap since I started writing. I wish I was kidding about that. Some days I wake up at four a.m. to write and some nights I stay up until midnight. Quite often my eyes, my rear, and my fingers ache.

I've had to work hard to fit in writing as I raised my four boys. I didn't want to miss out on time with them, so I work like a maniac when they're sleeping, at school, with friends, at church youth activities, or at lacrosse practice.

It's not easy to be a writing mama and I've made lots of mistakes in both. Sometimes I have no choice but to work when they're home and none of us like that very much. They are very patient with me but I know there are times they wished I wasn't a work-at-home mama. I don't think it's easy to be any kind of mama, but it's worth it. My boys are the most incredible people I know and bring me lots of joy.

Like most moms I struggle every day to find a balance, but I'm happy to say I have spent more hours teaching, loving, reading to, singing to, driving, cooking for, supporting at events, and playing with my boys than I have writing. Every minute spent with my boys is worth it, but sometimes it feels impossible and exhausting to juggle everything.

Finding a balance between family, work, church, service, friends, exercise, maintaining the house and yard, and a hundred other things isn't easy for any of us. Sometimes everything implodes and quite often I have to reevaluate and restructure time and demands. But if you're passionate about your children, your career, and your faith, and if you want to be successful, putting your best effort into each area of your life is essential.

The best advice a successful businesswoman and dear friend ever gave me was to be one hundred percent present in whatever you're doing. If you're with your family, focus on and enjoy them. If you're working, turn off the phone, TV, emails, or any other distractions. If you're playing, enjoy it to the fullest. Above all, don't waste time on meaningless activities that don't bring you joy. I guess if meaningless activities bring you joy, find a way to fit them into your day or your week.

I am a little OCD so I calendar my days, weeks, and months

and then I can focus on what I need to be doing at that moment. When I have free time, I can really enjoy it knowing I've taken care of my responsibilities or they are on the calendar for tomorrow. I can compartmentalize and deal with those items when they appear on my schedule. I try not to waste brain space on things that don't matter, don't help anyone, I can't change, or aren't on the agenda at that moment.

My husband and I tease about brain space a lot. I love to tell him, "Sorry sweetie, I don't have brain space for that." It's a standing joke with us, but I think it is truly important. Fill your brain with the important stuff. It is so easy to get distracted. My brain can get stewing on an issue with politics, family, lacrosse (very important to my boys and therefore to me) or any number of issues. But I have to stop and think about it. Can I fix whatever I'm stewing on? Will I do anything to fix it? If the answer to either is no, I replace it with something creative, uplifting, or inspiring.

You have to figure out what works for you, but for me, to get results, I have to be organized, focused, and present in that moment. And I absolutely cannot waste time because I don't have spare minutes in my day. I think most people are that way nowadays. We're all running faster than ever, so it's essential to eliminate the nonessentials.

The best advice I have on balance is to prioritize your time. Figure out what's really important to you. What do you think about when you let your mind wander and where do you spend your free time? If you're spending your free time playing games on your phone or watching Netflix, that's what you'll become an expert on. I spend my free time doing the things I love: being with my husband and boys, exercising, reading novels and scriptures, serving others, and writing.

Everybody has different ideas of free time. My husband loves playing pickle ball, golfing, boating, and watching Shark Tank. If my boys can't be on the ski slopes or on the lake, they are either outside playing lacrosse or, if the weather is bad, inside watching a college lacrosse game, even if said game was played two years ago. I'm more like Groucho Marx, who said, "I find television very educational; every time someone switches it on, I go into another room and read a good book."

My next piece of advice on getting stuff done you've heard often: put first things first. I start my day working out early, then focusing on my boys and husband until they're at work and school, and then I concentrate on getting words churned out or editing done. When I reach those goals, the boys are usually home from school, but every once in a while I get a minute to read my book, go visit somebody, or go on an extra walk.

It is so hard when you get distracted or interrupted with the endless appointments, phone calls, and even great things like serving others, church activities, or going to lunch with your family or friends. When those things are on my calendar—and honestly, most days something is—I work as hard as I can until I go and then when I get back I say a prayer and get back to work.

It's not easy to fit everything in. Sometimes we have to let things go. I have a driven personality and before my writing life, my house was very clean. Now my house is reasonably straightened, but definitely not deep cleaned, unless I hire a cleaning service.

At first that was hard on me, but I've seen the benefits of it as well. It doesn't bother me at all when something spills on the floor because the floor needs mopping anyway. Also, my boys and husband have stepped up to help. This was out of necessity, but they do a pretty great job. They do all nightly and dinner cleanup and load and unload dishes. When we aren't at games, work, church, on the boat, the slopes, the beach, or doing one of a hundred other activities, we work together to clean the house or do yard work. Several nights a week we gather around my bed and fold load upon load of laundry while we talk about our day.

The house isn't perfect, none of us are perfect, but it works for us and we get to spend more time together, so that's always a win.

I think the most important thing is finding a schedule that works for you and that you can be happy keeping, and try to smile and deal with it when the schedule gets thrown out of whack.

Chapter Two

MY WRITING PROCESS AND HOW TO BE A SPEED RACER

Work ethic, goal setting, and sacrifice are key to success.

My writing process has definitely changed over the years and drastically changed once my boys were all in school. When I tell people I write two books a month, their eyes bug out, but I have to explain that I have gradually gotten faster. I've been writing for almost twenty years and for the first fifteen years, I had at least one of my boys at home during the day and not much free time. If you are a young mom and anyone tells you it should be easy to fit writing time in because you're a stay-at-home mom, don't believe them. It's tough when they're little, they're adorable but busy and demanding, you're not sleeping, and your brain is mush.

Back to my writing process. My first few books each took me about a year to write. Gradually, I cut my time to a book every six months, then every four, every two, one a month, and finally to two books a month.

I learned how to write faster, but I also learned some valuable lessons. First, the more you do something, the faster you will get at it. I know that probably sounds stupid, but it's proven true for me. A book every two weeks might be insane to most people, but I have spent a lot of hours having stories spill out of my fingertips. That's not only made me a fast typist, despite having cut off three of my fingers in a lawnmower fourteen years ago, it has also trained my brain to process and create the story quickly. Also, when I'm immersed in a story, it's in my brain and part of my life and I don't have to relearn the story or who the characters are every time I pick it back up. I'm already there. If I take a few days off, it's rough because I have to go reread what I've done before I can progress. Staying in character is infinitely easier.

Two, you have to decide when your book, or whatever you are creating, is good enough. I kind of hate how that sounds because as an author I love, love what I do and I want every book to be a masterpiece. The problem is I am also a business-woman and my success has come from creating fabulous stories fast. The reason it took me a year to write each book at first was because I was learning and developing my talent, and my free time was short. It was also because I could spend a week getting one sentence perfect or coming up with the right word to make a scenery description jump off the page. Great stuff, and a jolly good time as a writer, but the perfect sentence doesn't really sell books.

I learned that for me developing awesome characters, witty dialogue, and lots of action sold stories. I've been told by many people that this is where my talent lies, so it was easier to lean that direction as well.

Often, I have to let go of perfection and focus on the story being there, let my editors help me develop it to the best book we have time for, and then sadly I have to let those friends go and move on to the next book. Luckily, I write series so I don't have to completely say goodbye too quick.

I have a side story, then I'll get back to my process and speedy writing. I met a couple of incredible guys, Daniel Coleman and Eric Bishop, at a League of Utah Writers meeting when I was first starting out. The three of us started going to each other's houses once a week and critiquing five pages from each of our stories. Learning from Eric and Daniel is one of the keys to me writing well. I honestly wonder how I was so blessed to have them include me in their group. They are both fabulous writers and brilliant men with impressive and diverse backgrounds.

We'd been working together for almost a year when Eric basically said to me, "Cami, you're an amazing writer and you need to focus on literary fiction. Forget this romantic suspense and these fluff stories."

I was flattered, because honestly we're all so hard on ourselves and I've never thought of myself as some "amazing writer." But I knew literary fiction wasn't my path. I told him thank you for the compliment, but I absolutely loved romantic suspense and I would probably wither up and quit writing if I had to write literary fiction. Writing scenery and description is still the hardest part of any book for me.

About eight years later, our little group had long since dissolved. Daniel had become, and still is, my favorite editor, and I hadn't seen Eric in a while. I was speaking at a conference on how to produce fast fiction and Eric came to my class. I was finished with the presentation and doing a Q&A when Eric stood up and told everyone in the class how he tried to convince me to write literary fiction and I told him in no uncertain terms that wasn't my path. He then told the class that I had been right, I'd known where my passion and talents were, and look at the success I'd had.

I can't tell you how much I appreciate those two men and all they taught and did for me, but also recognizing that I had followed my path. Though no path is easy or straight or not full of rocks and scratchy weeds, my path is turning out the way I wanted it to.

Okay, back to the process.

Three, series are where it is at for writing fast. I love series and luckily my readers do as well. There is a little more legwork up front, figuring out location, family, names, overall conflict, basic plots, careers, etc. If you want to see me biting all my fingernails and downing chocolate, come to my house on a day I'm setting up a series.

I try not to stress about knowing everything and having the set up be perfect. It's hard not to, but I'm coming to recognize that most stuff can be changed or tweaked. Especially if you're a write by the seat of your pants kind of girl like I am.

One side note—I couldn't have set up an entire series as a newer author. I actually remember when I'd done a few stand-alones, and I met the group of incredible ladies who would be my favorite author friends. Somebody said we should do a series together. I was stoked about it, and we started our Snow Valley Romances, but I remember saying to them time and again when they'd ask me for a blurb or even a title for my upcoming book, "I can't focus on anything but the book I'm writing right now. I don't have head space for that!"

They were always sweet about it, but now I know you have to be well versed in story structure, characterization, and the overall picture before you can crank out series. We all learn and improve, me slower than most, but it comes as you put in the work time and time again.

The great thing about series is once you've got covers, titles, books up for preorder, setting, premise, and a lot of your characters' names, you can churn those books out. It's much easier to write books two through ten as you already have ideas coming from the previous books and they layer and build on each other. It's also a lot of fun. My husband teases me that most people don't wake up on Monday morning gleefully rubbing their hands together because they get to work. We authors, and anyone who loves their work, are very blessed.

Fourth, there is a time and a season for everything. Over the years, I have learned a lot and increased my speed. I could not have written two books a month while I had a baby or toddler. I guess I could have, but I would've missed out on my cute boys. My four boys are each over four years apart in age, so I was in the baby and toddler stage for a while. When they were little, I was lucky to get a short amount of writing time during naps, or if they slept in and I got my workout finished early and still had a minute to write. I also tried to write at night, but I was usually too exhausted. I also traded with my sweet sister-in-law babysitting and that was fun to have the cousins together and gave me a little extra time.

My writing process, and schedule, as of today, goes something like this. I work six days a week.

Monday through Friday, I wake up early to work out and then spend time with my boys before school. I write like a madwoman for the six hours my boys are in school. Every time I hit a thousand words or if I'm editing when I get through a chapter, I take a break to do some exercises and stretch, check emails and texts, deal with any marketing stuff, and then I'm back to work.

When my boys get home, I'm a mom again. Sometimes it is tough. You've probably been there—you're in the middle of an incredible scene or you're three hundred words from your goal and the alarm goes off to pick up carpool or the teenager drives up. That's when I fake it till I make it, put a smile on my face, and quickly remember they're my top priority. I can get the writing done later.

I get extra work time in when they're at a friend's house, church activities, or lacrosse practice. On Saturdays, I work the three hours my boys are working as janitors cleaning my husband's building, and sometimes I work from nine p.m. to midnight on Saturday night if I'm really behind. Sundays, I never work. I don't respond to emails on Sundays, check my ranking, or do any kind of writing work. My brain needs the rest as much as my spirit needs to be renewed.

So six days a week, I either produce five thousand words per day, sometimes more if I get behind or we've been on vacation, or I edit. Each morning before I produce words, I go back and read the five thousand words from the day before so it's all fresh in my mind. I give myself about an hour to do the read-through, make some edits along the way, and then start adding to it. I can write a thousand words in forty minutes, so I have a twenty-minute break every hour to deal with other stuff. And if I stay on schedule, I'm done producing by the time the boys get home.

My books are usually forty to fifty thousand words. I can get a book written in ten days and then I read through the entire thing before sending it to my content or development editor. I start on the next book while I wait about a week to get the previous book back. When the book comes back from the editor, I take a break from my current WIP and implement the developmental edits, read through the book and improve it, and then send it on to my copy or proof editor. Then I go right back to creating words for my book in progress. When I get copy edits back, I take a break to accept all of those changes, do a final proof, and then I format and upload the book, and get back to creating. Yes, sometimes I feel like a ping-pong ball. It's tough to keep all the characterization straight. I do have a file of notes on characters that I update regularly so I can refer to that, but usually a few pages into each story, I'm right back with my buddies and focused on them.

One side note on how I work—I create the story sitting on my cozy couch with my feet up, tapping away on my laptop. I edit on my desk treadmill, usually walking pretty slowly, but I keep moving or I'll either fall asleep or bite off all my fingernails. I do all marketing, emails, and zoom calls with my ad agency or other business calls at my standup desk.

A good friend, teacher, and motivator was asking me about this part of my process, and he was stoked about what I shared. He told me that was exactly what he tries to teach his students. If you can train your brain to compartmentalize and know when you're in a certain spot, and at certain times of the day, you'll be accomplishing a certain task, it will make you faster and more effective at each task. I didn't realize I was doing that, but I wish I would've known that years ago and I would've compartmentalized a lot sooner.

Any questions? Email me at cami@camichecketts.com. I'd love to hear from you and to expound on anything or hear how your process works. I'm always excited to learn and change.

Isn't that what life—and the writing process—is about? Learning, changing, developing, tweaking, realizing what works and honing in on that, realizing what doesn't work and changing it.

The one constant we can plan on is change. I've learned never to get too set in my ways or overconfident that I'm doing it "right." Change is hard but good and usually it makes us better and more resilient.

Be open to new ideas. Be open to change. Be open to improving. At the same time, trust yourself and your process and don't go chasing every new idea or whim in the publishing industry. Figure out what works for you and make gradual changes that improve upon that.

Being a speed racer has been one of my keys to success, but it might not be yours. I can think of many things that are more important than speed: consistency, believing in yourself, writing friends, supportive family, and not giving up, to name a few.

Figure out what you're good at and lean toward those strengths. We all have to improve on our weaknesses as well, but be careful not to beat yourself up or beat your head against a wall. Focus on the positive and never ever quit and good things will follow.

Chapter Three

WHERE DO ALL THE IDEAS COME FROM?

Get your butt in the chair and the ideas will come.

New ideas and creativity have been a progression for me, like everything else in my journey. Twenty years ago, I had so many stories in my head and I felt like a lot of characters almost lived up there.

My sister told me a while ago that she'd had a miserable run because her headphones died and she couldn't listen to music. I looked at her strangely and said, "Why didn't you just talk to all the people in your head?"

"Cam ..." She shook her head and tried to explain, "Most of us don't have people talking in our heads." Then she made a signal I think means crazy. Not sure really.

I don't know which one of us is more normal. Okay, I can guess it's probably my sis. But as an author, I used to love the people in my head. They told me stories. They gave me funny lines. They kept me from ever being bored on a run. I actually blame them for cutting my fingers off in the lawnmower. I was busy arguing with a character in a story.

Maybe all of these conversations was just me talking to myself, or maybe I had multiple personalities or something, but it helped a lot with story creation.

As I've written more and more, or maybe just as I've gotten older and have hardly any free time to let my mind wander, I don't hear voices anymore. I usually brainstorm and come up with an opening scene for a book. Then I kneel and pray for help and inspiration and I sit down and get to work. The ideas come as I'm writing. Sometimes ideas will randomly come throughout my day, but it's mostly when I'm working on and immersed in the story.

Nightmares used to be a source of inspiration when I first started out. I wrote as therapy for postpartum and for my nightmares. Yes, I need a real therapist, but I'm too cheap.

I still have nightmares and sometimes I use them. Often they are too disturbing or violent to write about. I'll know I can use a nightmare if I can tell someone else about it without them visibly cringing or staring at me like I'm a raving lunatic. But even my awful nightmares give me inspiration for how a character would feel in a terrifying situation.

Doing mundane tasks often gets the creative juices flowing. I love running and have spent many miles composing stories or scenes. The only problem is when I get home and I can't quite make it sound as good as it did in my head. Then I have to keep revising it until it works. I also get revelation scrubbing toilets. It's a very inspiring spot with four boys who don't aim well.

As I've written more and more books, and am on a tight publication schedule, I can't wait for inspiration. Now I go with the good old fashioned: Get your butt in the chair and the ideas will come.

This has been consistently true for me. The ideas flow as I'm writing, as I'm putting in the time, as I'm letting my rear grow and eating lots of chocolate. As I spend that time with my characters and my story, I know them better than ever and I know what they need and what needs to happen.

The more words I put down, the more inspiration comes. Sometimes I have to cut scenes that went the wrong direction, or my mean editor tells me I need to wring out more emotion or stop leaving writing gold off the page, but the more I write it seems the less time I waste going the wrong direction.

The inspiration is obviously not from me, but from above. I am so grateful for the ideas and light my Father above gives me. As I pray for help, and put in the time working, I receive more and more ideas and my gratitude for Him grows.

Some people feel it's weak to rely on heaven for help. I had someone tell me once, "You need your little religion crutch because you're not as smart as me."

I'm so grateful I'm not as smart as that person, and I really like being weak. I couldn't get through one hour without the light and strength from heaven above.

"Every good gift and every perfect gift is from above, and cometh down from the Father of lights, with whom is no variableness, neither shadow of changing." James 1:17

Chapter Four

WHY DO YOU WRITE?

If I can make one person happy with my writing, I will feel it is a success.

I write because I can't stop. Honestly, I just love it. I know I'm an addictive-type personality because writing, exercise, and chocolate are impossible for me to give up.

I feel strongly that writing is a calling for me. It's a talent I've been given and I've been blessed to have the time and opportunity to develop my talent and share clean and Christian fiction with the world. I hope what I am sharing brings light and inspiration.

Years ago, a close friend called me and expressed heartfelt concern that I was writing too fast and spending too much time writing. I really appreciated her caring enough to share her concerns with me and I immediately went to my Heavenly Father in prayer. The answer I received was, *I gave you this talent —you use it.*

That's a sacred experience for me and I don't want to cheapen that by sharing it casually, but I felt I could share it here. I feel strongly that we can each have the answers and inspiration we personally need if we obey God's laws and ask for inspiration and light in our lives. He is waiting to help you. He lives and He loves us. Of course He will help and inspire you if you humbly ask.

I also write because of my fans. I have the coolest readers in the world and their emails, messages on social media, reviews, and support make such a difference to me. Over the twenty years of my writing journey, hundreds upon hundreds of people have personally thanked me for writing or told me how much one of my books helped them. I'm extremely humbled to have been able to share my light with them.

A personal story before I move on.

My oldest son loves to read my books. He is a tall, tough lacrosse player and in high school, his buddies would tease him about reading romance. He'd just give this cute little grin and say, "That's why I get all the ladies."

When he was a junior, he had the awful experience of reading a book assigned for school about a child trained to kill and be a warrior. It disturbed him, but he hadn't told anyone. His friends and I had no idea what was going on. We just knew something was off and he was grumpy.

He came home early one weekend night and then I was even more worried. I didn't understand why he wasn't with his friends. I tried to get him to talk to me, but he asked me to please give him a few hours alone. Two hours later, he came running into the kitchen, picked me up off my feet, gave me a big squeeze and said, "Thank you, Mama. I was so ticked off about this awful book I had to read for school, but I just re-read *Shadows in the Curtain* and now I'm happy again."

You can imagine that I cried. If I can make one person happy with my writing I will feel it is a success, but especially if I can make my sweet boy happy.

Chapter Five

GETTING PUBLISHED AND THE MOVE TO INDIE OR SELF-PUBLISHING

For me, it is worth it to put in the work to be a one-woman publishing house in exchange for freedom, independence, and a lot higher income.

A quick timeline to begin this chapter. I started writing in 2002 and started sending books to agents and publishers shortly after. I'm sure they got a good laugh out of my queries and sample chapters. I was rejected and rejected and rejected. My husband held me while I cried about it. He stopped letting me get the mail after a while. Can you believe in 2002 we were still getting good old-fashioned mail? The only good part was my boys liked to help me burn rejection letters. You can't do that with email.

I didn't give up. I never even thought of giving up. I attended conferences, writing workshops, any writing meeting I could find, joined critique groups in person and online, read books and articles on writing, entered contests on writing, and basically did everything I could think of to improve my writing.

After five years of learning and getting rejected, my first two books were published in 2007 with a small publishing house. They were very nice people, but didn't have much budget for marketing. They also didn't have great contacts with brick and mortar bookstores and this was long before ebooks or audio books were getting any traction.

On a side note, in 2007 I also chopped off three of my fingers in a lawnmower. So it was a pretty hard year of recuperation and after the torturous pain of desensitizing the reattached fingers, I had to teach myself how to type again. I can't blame that publisher for the books not succeeding like we'd hoped since was the Brainiac who was daydreaming with my characters and stuck my hand in a lawnmower.

My third book, *The Sister Pact*, was published in 2009 with a much larger publishing house, and I was thrilled. I spent a lot of my 2009 writing time doing book signings, speaking engagements, blog tours, and anything else the mighty publishers asked me to do. I thought I'd arrived. Even family members who had questioned my dedication to writing thought I'd arrived.

I sent my next book to my publisher, and they said *The Sister Pact* was going so well they wanted to slow down and wait a year before publishing another one. That made absolutely no sense to me. I am first and foremost a reader. And I know as a reader what I want—I want a huge pile books waiting to be read from the authors I enjoy.

But the publishers were the experts. So I kept writing when I could but mostly did book signings and speaking engagements and focused on my boys.

At the beginning of 2010, my publisher emailed me and shared the great news that I was one of their bestsellers of 2009. I was so stoked. I'd gotten one paycheck from them and had honestly been a little disappointed, but obviously more was coming. Right?

The answer was no, not much more was coming. As a "bestseller," I had sold over five thousand print copies at eighteen dollars per copy. I made almost seventy cents on every copy sold. So in 2009, I made thirty-five hundred dollars. I wasn't writing for the money. I love to write. But chasing around doing book signings and speaking and attending functions while missing time with my boys to only make thirty-five hundred dollars over the course of a year was absolutely sickening to me.

About this same time, I was part of a fabulous writing group of about ten local writers. The afore-mentioned Daniel Coleman was in the group, and I got to complaining and sharing my disappointment.

He said to me, "Why don't you look at self-publishing?"

I kind of recoiled. I was traditionally published and had gained a lot of respect from my book being on the shelves of huge bookstores and speaking and signing all over the place. Self-publishing was looked down on and honestly I didn't have the writing budget to produce my own covers, do my own marketing, pay someone to format my books, or take any other risks like that.

Luckily, I have an absolutely incredible husband who is also an entrepreneur. He supported me, acted as my sounding board, and gave me ideas. At the time, I was also having success incorporating my fitness background with writing and was making decent money writing fitness articles for a Christian magazine. So I saved every bit of that money and my whopping thirty-five hundred from my "big-time" publisher, and I went to work.

It wasn't easy. It wasn't fast. There were almost as many tears as back in the early days of being rejected by agents and publishers alike. There were moments I thought I'd figured things out and then I'd have a setback.

One of these moments was in January of 2012 when I asked for my rights back from my first publisher on *The Broken Path*. I'd heard about a crazy idea of putting a book for free on Amazon for five days before you did the official book launch. I had a sweet friend take pictures for the cover and my brother-in-law, niece, and another friend were my models. I proofed the previously published book (no money for edits) and tried it out.

The Broken Path hit #2 in the overall free store on Amazon. After the five free days, it transferred automatically to #2 in the paid store on Amazon, then gradually dropped in ranking over the next few weeks.

As a newbie to self-publishing and Amazon, I had absolutely no clue how great that was. Until I received a bank deposit from Amazon for twenty-thousand dollars and realized I'd sold over ten thousand copies.

You can imagine I was stoked. I was sure I had it all figured out. I put most of that money in the writing fund (only bought a couple fun dresses and a few things for my boys), wrote another book as fast as I could, with my husband helping with the boys whenever he could, hired a cover artist and paid editors, and in April I put out *Poison Me*.

I used the brilliant five days free strategy.

This book release was nothing like the previous one. Truthfully, it was awful. Amazon had changed their algorithms (I know, shocking) and when a book moved from the free store to the paid store, the ranking dropped to the millions and the book had to fight its way up from the bottom. I had done absolutely nothing else to market. I had a few faithful followers, but definitely not enough to overcome a horrible release. The book flopped.

I had to start all over with good old hard work and lots and lots of prayer for inspiration. Luckily, I had saved most of the money from *The Broken Path* release so I could keep my writing alive until I figured it out.

As a busy mama of four, I could not waste time chasing ideas that didn't work. I promise you the Lord has inspired me with ideas for plots and characterization to create the books, but also for marketing strategies and, most importantly, He has placed wonderful authors and editors in my life to help me.

I kept writing and producing books. I worked hard to build up my social media and newsletter list. I exchanged shout-outs with other authors. I kept going to writing conferences and retreats when I could afford it. I exchanged critiques with anybody and everybody because I was trying to save my money and only pay for final round edits. I researched bloggers and was able to get featured and grow my audience through sending the bloggers free books and doing interviews. I organized prize give-aways with willing companies to grow my fan base on social media and my newsletter subscribers.

Like any self-employed person, I spent years trying to grow my brand, figure out my niche, and put out a quality product consistently.

Then in 2014, something life changing happened. I went to an indie author conference with some friends from my small valley, but I was too cheap to pay for the eighteen-dollar lunch. An author I'd met at a book signing back in the book signing days asked me to walk to a nearby bakery. There, I met five incredible ladies and at that very lunch we created Snow Valley and ended up writing five anthologies together. We shared everything, most importantly our followers, and it was a pivotal point for my writing success.

By about 2017, I was producing a book every two to three months. Some of my series had done well, particularly my Billionaire Bride Pact series that I wrote with Jeanette Lewis. I was developing a fan base, mostly because of my author group and the awesome theory of Taylor Hart: "You lift me, I lift you, and we'll all ascend together." I'll talk more about the crucial aspect of writing support and friends in a few chapters.

At this point I was making money, but not a huge amount. As authors, we write because we love it, but if you aren't making a living doing it, it will be very hard to keep spending a significant amount of time writing.

Here's how my pivotal moment happened. My youngest son, Phoenix—call sign Pizza, Mr. Adorable and Hilarious and everybody's favorite smart aleck—was starting first grade. I would now have six hours a day to focus on writing. I told my husband if I didn't make X amount the first month Pizza went to school all day, I would get a job using my degree. I knew I could make that amount working full-time as a personal trainer.

I had no desire to put my writing on the back burner because it was my passion, but I'd been writing part-time for fifteen years at this point and it was time to see if this could be a successful career or if it needed to just be a hobby.

I'm happy to report that the first month Pizza was in first grade, I made double the amount I'd set. I earmarked writing as my career, knew I could be successful at it, and my income and audience have only gone up since.

I'm pretty quiet about what I make. My husband teases me that it's a catch-22. Instinctively you want people to know you're successful, but you never want to brag or create jealous or competitive feelings in others. I will say that I feel extremely blessed to be successful at a job I love and I have been able to donate generously to various charities while making a huge difference for our family's income as well.

For me, self-publishing has been incredible and a lot of work. I love being my own boss. Yes, I put in a lot of hours and my work is never done. I can sneak into the office at two a.m. to deal with something. I wear a lot of hats but I have the freedom to do what I want and publish what I want, when I want. I get to choose my hours and my deadlines. I get to choose my own fabulous editors and cover designers, social media people, and ad team.

I am responsible for my own success and there is an immense feeling of accomplishment to be a self-made success story. I am very grateful for my path and especially for Heavenly Father's help and inspiration along the way and the wonderful people who've walked the path with me.

Chapter Six

DEVELOPING YOUR WRITING SUPPORT TEAM

inding people who support your writing and finding the right professionals to work with is a huge deal for writing success.

For me, finding the right people was right up there on my list of keys to success right under *don't let rejection stop you* and *butt in chair, hands on keyboard.*

It doesn't happen overnight. Finding my loyal and incredible author friends took years and years of writing conferences, writing groups, writing meetings, and writing retreats to develop.

I feel I've found the best people as I hustle and work hard and also as I want their success as much as I want my own and give back to them.

My husband and I have the blessing and opportunity of working with the college-aged youth in our church calling. They are amazing. They give us renewed faith in the future of our world. We often get questions on dating. The one piece of advice I hear myself saying often is: become the type of person you want to marry and you will probably find that person.

I feel the same advice applies to finding writing friends: work hard, be generous, look for success and share it, and the writing friends you're hoping for will gravitate to you.

I'm going to list my people and some thoughts about each of them.

My mom.

She thinks I'm amazing, which I appreciate and need. I don't know that any of us are to the level our mom thinks we are, but it's very motivating to have someone who believes in you without a doubt. She hands my business cards to everyone she meets and is so proud. I'm sure some people she's met shake their heads at this overzealous mama. For me, she is the most adorable, sweet mama on the planet. I hope everyone has someone like my mom in their lives.

My husband.

He's an absolute stud. For almost twenty years he's supported me, even when my dream was costing us money. I asked him once why he'd done that. He said first of all because he loves me, but second because he could see how happy my writing made me and the confidence it gave me.

Like I said—absolute stud. He takes the boys to do fun things when I'm on a deadline. He brings me takeout when I don't have time to cook. He listens to my crazy ideas and only teases me occasionally about telling Peter Pan and the Tooth Fairy hi when they fly by. He runs errands, cooks, and hires someone to clean to free up my time to write. I don't have to daydream up heroes for my novels. I live with one.

I know not everyone has a supportive spouse like Stan. Every marriage and relationship is different and it doesn't help to compare, but I have to give my honey kudos for being awesome. I pray I give to my husband like he gives to me. I try, but I'm afraid I come up short often.

I've watched author friends whose spouses were not supportive. I think everyone tries to be supportive, but a writer's work is demanding and solitary and it can be a long road to success. I'm not sure what advice to give except to be patient and try to put family first so nobody feels neglected. That's probably the hardest thing about writing—stepping out of my imaginary world and making sure my real people are feeling lots of love from me.

My author friends.

These ladies are such a blessing in my life. I tear up just thinking about them. They truly get me. I love my "real life" friends completely, but when I talk about the best way to kill a mafia guy or how to make my black moment blacker or how sick I am of finding new ways to describe a kiss, most people in my real world get a very blank expression.

My author friends not only understand, but they brainstorm everything from plot lines to marketing, cheer for my successes, humor me by going on walks at author retreats, and love me completely. We laugh and dance and work so hard together. I love every moment I am able to spend with them.

It took me almost as many years to develop the deep friendships I have with my author friends as it did to make significant money at writing. If you're still developing your group, don't stress and don't give up. It is so worth it.

Side note—you can find author friends at writing conferences, workshops, retreats, critique exchange, writers' meetings, and book signings. Sometimes you can pick them up online, but it is infinitely better to hang out in person, give hugs, and share your chocolate.

My editors.

So much love for my editors. I hope that doesn't make it weird as they read this. My content editor is like a brother. He can make fun of me (maybe tease sounds better) and give me a hard time and I can just laugh at him and know he does it to make the book better. I would be nowhere close to my level of success without the knowledge, expertise, and pushing (sometimes shoving) of my content editor.

My copy editor is an angel and is very good at making me look good. I love her.

Finding editors is tough. I started with the free route of critique exchanges. That was great for a while, but other authors are not always great editors. Honestly, I am not a great editor. I'm not even a subpar editor. Part of the reason for that is I have a hard time being critical and I worry a lot about offending someone. The other problem for me with critique exchanges was the time it took out of my valuable writing time.

From critique exchanges, I tried out many editors. It was hard for me to find editors who improved my book and pushed me as a writer but weren't snarky and belittling. Honestly, I went through some editors who were so snarky I'd walk away from the edit hating my own book and thinking I was a waste of skin. Luckily, I was confident enough to realize they weren't the right fit and move on quick.

It's also hard to find editors who can edit as fast as I need. Most are not a week turnaround. I've been blessed with editors who are willing to focus solely on my book. I think that's partially because I schedule my edits in advance and I always stick to my deadlines, and partially because I don't mind paying for quality work.

My ad guys.

It has only been in the past couple of years that I could afford an ad agency. When I first started, I couldn't even afford an ad budget. Then for many years I threw ad money at Amazon and Facebook and prayed it did something.

I lucked into a referral to my ad agency from my impressive friends who own Nani Swimwear.

My ad guys are incredible and they save me so much time and stress. I'm so grateful not to spend the time, energy, and head space on ads. The fact that they are experts at Amazon and Facebook is invaluable. Each of them respectively worked previously at Amazon and Facebook, so you can imagine they have inside knowledge I'll never have or want to have. Their ad creation and success is miles beyond the days when I used to create ads and hope something worked.

My social media people.

They're so cute. My sister and two of my boys. We're definitely not experts at social media, but I like having a reason to pay them to help me and I honestly haven't seen social media make that much difference in monetary return. I think it's important to have a presence on most platforms, but I don't see a huge jump in return from social media posts. I try to keep them fun, a way to connect with my readers, do giveaways, to get my name out there and increase awareness of my brand.

My readers.

I love the gracious, incredible, smart people who read my books, connect with my characters, and are so kind to me. So much love and gratitude for every one of them.

I'm forgetting some people.

Oh yeah ... *my awesome boys and daughter-in-law*. They're my favorite people on the planet. I love any chance I have to be around them. They give me so many funny one-liners and ideas and they give me lots of hugs and are super proud of me. So grateful for my family, and I try every day to give back to them what they give to me.

Chapter Seven

THE EXERCISE ANGLE – HOW DO YOU FIT IT IN AND DOES BEING HEALTHY HELP YOUR SUCCESS?

Even ten minutes to get the body moving and the blood pumping can help the brain function better with increased blood flow and get the creative juices flowing.

I'll try to keep this chapter short and not make it an infomercial on exercise. But I have to say yes, exercise and being healthy will make a huge difference in anyone's success.

Here are just a few of the benefits besides weight loss, improved muscle strength and tone, and feeling and looking great.

Exercise reduces the risk of disease so you can keep working now and in the future; improves mental health and mood; helps keep your thinking, learning, and judgment skills sharp as you age; enhances quality of sleep; decreases stress levels; increases energy; improves self-esteem; and improves discipline and productivity.

It has been proven that people who are fit are more successful.

I love brainstorming while I run, walk, bike, lift weights, or swim. I have complete scenes come to me sometimes. I believe movement opens your mind to process any kind of problem or kick up the creative juices.

I also have to tout that even though I spend an hour or more a day exercising, I have seen that I get more accomplished in a day. I have to believe that's because exercise gives me energy and focus.

If you want to test the theory, find something active you enjoy doing and add it to your day. See how it affects you. It doesn't have to be a significant amount of time. Even ten minutes to get the body moving and the blood pumping can help the brain function better with increased blood flow and get the creative juices flowing as well.

Chapter Eight

MARKETING AND WHAT'S WORKING CURRENTLY TO SELL BOOKS

hange will come; adapt to it, try new things, keep going forward. The only constant is change. What works today might change tomorrow, as evidenced by my success with *The Broken Path* that I couldn't replicate.

Sometimes that stinks, you finally figure out how an ad works, or discover a great promo site that actually sells books, and then it changes. But sometimes change gives us the opportunity to develop our career and try something new.

I'm not one that loves change. In my dream world, I'd just write the stories that come to me and not deal with all the rest. None of us live in that dream world, so I'll try to share the things that have worked for me to hit the level of income I have and that seem to be currently working.

Kindle Unlimited.

I make between seventy to eighty percent of my income from Kindle Unlimited, Amazon's lending library where authors get paid for each page read.

I resisted joining for a while because I'm not a fan of monopolies. Honestly, I only shop at my local grocery store and try to resist big business. But Taylor Hart called me out and told me I was missing out. I needed to get on and "ride the wave." She was right. I do still have some of my books out on all platforms, but most of my books are currently exclusive to Amazon.

I love KU as a reader as well. I borrow a lot of books and usually only read the first five to ten pages of most of them. It's incredible research for me to find what actually draws me in as a reader. Do you remember reading Donald Maass's *First Five Pages*? Back when I was dying for an agent, I thought it was ludicrous that they could claim to read less than five pages and know if the book was sellable. Now I totally believe it. If the author doesn't capture me quick, I'm gone, and I don't think I'm alone on that.

Ads.

It's tough to know where to put ad money. The only tried and true that have worked for me are Facebook and Amazon ads. I'm cautious about putting too much money into either. Facebook ads can drive Amazon rankings in the right direction, but I haven't always seen the financial return. Amazon ads seem to do better if they run longer. That's a problem for me as I produce so quickly and I want to focus my ad money on new releases. My ad guys have gradually talked me into advertising a variety of different books, mostly first in the series and books that have been consistent bestsellers. We are seeing the payoff for that.

If you're doing your ads yourself, plan on spending time each day looking at your performance, click-through, negative keywords, search terms, and adjusting as you need. When I did my own ads, I tried to focus on getting my words written for the day first because ad managing can suck my creativity fast. It's a necessary evil, though. Even if you're only spending a small amount, I believe having ads running is important. I've been impressed with how well my ad guys can stretch a dollar. I'm spending a quarter of what I used to on ads and seeing higher returns. But it has only been the past couple of years that I could justify hiring an ad agency. If you're not to that point, there are classes online and at conferences that teach you how to maximize ad spend and reach, or if you're like me and hate sitting through classes, you can try a bunch of low budget ads, play around and see what works. From what I understand, the easiest is a sponsored brand with automatic targeting. My ad guy was explaining recently that he uses the automatic targeting (basically the Amazon ad bots target the ads for you) to find words and targets and mine information for other ads.

I spend the bulk of my ad spend on new releases. It seems that everybody wants the shiny new penny, and as a reader I totally get this. I don't want to hear about a book I read a year ago. I want my favorite authors to have something new for me to read.

My ad guys also set up different ads on my current or upcoming series preorders. That gets the ads running and gives my guys time to tweak the keywords, data, search terms, ad copy, and for Facebook, the graphics that bring in the highest click through. Then a few days before release, we up the spend on a particular book. A few days after release, we taper down and get ready to focus on the next book in a series.

They also talk a lot about "brand defense," which basically means you pay to protect your name. It bothers me that I'm paying for Cami Checketts because in my mind, if somebody types in Cami Checketts they're looking for me and should find me. I was proven wrong a year before I signed up with my ad agency. My income was dipping because everybody else was targeting my name except for me. It turns out that readers might type in my name and then click on the first book they see, which might or might not be my book. If I'm not willing to pay for that top spot, it probably wasn't my book they clicked on. Brand defense is expensive and annoying to me, but I recognize now I have to do it.

We have tried Google ads and BookBub ads. Honestly I'm not doing either at this point as I've never seen a boost in sales or overall income from them. BookBub Featured Deals are a different story and are invaluable, if you can get one. I get rejected often for those, makes me nostalgic for old days of being rejected by publishers. BookBub New Release for Less deals I have not seen to be effective but I've only done them at a $4.99 price point. A discounted price might be more effective.

There are a lot of different book promotion sites. I have not tried all of them but I've tried my fair share. The only ones I've seen to give enough bump in sales to justify their cost are Ereader News Today and Robin Reads. There are probably other amazing sites out there, but most have not given me much of a return.

Publishing quick and on a schedule.

Not everyone can write and produce quick. Don't beat yourself up if you're not as fast as you want to be. I think it's just as important that you publish on a schedule. Especially if you're doing KU and are exclusive to Amazon. Amazon's bots seem to favor the consistent release. One thing I've noticed is that as I consistently produce, my ranking starts in a better spot on release day than it used to.

Publish a book every month, every few months, or every six

months. Figure out what works for you, your sanity, schedule, and demands with your family and life. I would suggest calendaring it and sticking to your release date. As I mentioned, setting deadlines and sticking to them is something I do religiously. The authors who push back release dates risk upsetting the bots, but more importantly upsetting their faithful readers.

Preorders.

A few years ago, preorders didn't work for me. It was far too restrictive and stressful. Currently I think it's awesome. As I get a series lined up and the preorders come in, I'm assured that money. KU is great, but I make more if someone buys the book outright at $4.99 and I don't have to worry if they stop turning pages.

Also, when that preorder money lands in my account I get a huge boost in income. Right now, it seems the Amazon bots like preorders and the more preorder numbers I have, the more favorable my ranking will be on release day. I usually have my book release one day before launch day when I announce it to my readers.

My book releases, the preorders get sent out, and the ranking drops closer to the number one spot, the momentum building for the next twenty-four hours. Then I send out newsletters, post on social media, increase ad spend, etc., to really have the release take off and have a successful launch day.

Audiobooks.

I currently only have six audiobooks that I've produced on my own using narrators I chose through ACX, and I have twenty-nine audiobooks produced by a major audiobook publisher. Neither have been huge returns for me. I've only earned out my advances with the publisher on twelve of the twenty-nine books and they've been available for a few years now. The nice thing with the large audiobook publisher is I didn't have to pay for narration or find the narrators. The drawback is I doubt I'll ever make much money on them.

Some of my friends are having success paying for a narrator and then putting the audiobooks for sale on the various audio platforms but also putting audiobooks up on YouTube for free to become monetized through YouTube.

For me it hasn't been worth the money spent on narration, but as my ad guys are constantly reminding me, it's important to have a presence on all platforms so when somebody types your name into YouTube, TikTok, Instagram, Google, or wherever, your stuff actually comes up, not pirated versions or other people getting exposure by using your name.

My thoughts on audio right now are it's a great idea to have that option. Some readers seem to love audiobooks. I personally am not spending a bunch of money or time on audiobooks. I have three reasons for that. One: I don't have the time with my family and writing schedule. Two: I'm not seeing the financial return. Three: with the way technology is going, there are already different ways available for readers to have their ebooks read aloud to them or digital narration that is getting better and better. I believe that technology will keep improving on these options and soon producing audiobooks with a narrator will not be worth it for the indie author.

We'll see. I've been wrong before. Actually, lots of times. Don't tell my boys.

Newsletter and newsletter exchanges.

A newsletter is the best marketing tool an author can have. It takes a lot of time and patience to build up a great newsletter following, but then it's basically free. I've done a lot of different things to build my newsletter—links to download a free book when they sign up on my website and in every book I sell; give-aways with the entry being signing up; BookFunnel promos; Ryan Zee promos; Facebook ads. You name it, I've probably tried it and gradually I've built up an awesome follower.

Newsletter exchanges are usually done with people in your genre that you trust will send out your information to their entire list. Sometimes authors segment their list so their news-letter exchange is not that effective for you. For the most part, I only exchange newsletters with people I know and trust. If they say they will give my book an exclusive newsletter, meaning my book, cover, excerpt, banner, and links are the only thing in the newsletter, I know they will do it. I've also been burned before trying to be kind and send out an author's book and that author is not the level of clean or sweet that my audience expects. If you don't have time to read something the author has written, I'd be careful about exchanging. You're basically endorsing that book and you want to make sure not to upset your readers.

I believe newsletter exchanges have helped me get to the level of income and readership that I have. My fabulous group of author friends have gone through different phases with exchanging newsletters—sending out huge blasts at a certain time, staggering newsletters, doing exclusives or putting the featured author at the "top of the page"—it has all been helpful for release days, book sales, and most importantly increasing our followers and audience.

Currently, I don't do many exchanges. It got to a point where my newsletter was looking like an ad and not a newsletter. Also, I no longer see much of a bump in sales or downloads when another author sends my book out in their newsletter. I assume this is because most of my author friends have a similar fan base.

It's probably more annoying than anything for our readers to see the same book from several authors on the same day.

But as we were growing our readership, it was essential to do exchanges. If a friend asks, I still do them. I always want to help out if I can and I believe there's still value exchanging if it's not overdone.

I also slowed down exchanging because of the following story.

About eight months ago, I was on a Zoom call with my ad guys and they asked how often I sent my newsletter—once a month, once a week?

At that point in time, I was still doing a lot of exchanges and I squeaked out in response, "Um ... five, six days a week."

There was a shocked silence, and then they kindly suggested I cut back to once, maybe twice a week.

It was brutal, but I'm finally there. They explained that it's not only a matter of annoying readers with constant newsletters and getting unsubscribes, but the more often you send newsletters, Gmail or Yahoo will send you straight to the spam folder and your readers won't even see all those well-crafted emails. I'm not sure if that always happens or if it depends on your email service, number of subscribers, or the current moon cycle (honestly, don't you sometimes feel like there are a lot of mysteries in marketing?), but I will say my unsubscribes are substantially lower with less emails going out and my opens and click rates are much, much higher than they've ever been. The other nice thing is I'm not wasting time organizing and sending out all those emails.

These are the best tips I have as of right now. As trends change, I'll update the book.

Now I feel it's time to share my Sinclair analogy.

In my little town, we have a Sinclair gas station with a grill. Their food is unbelievably good, fresh, inexpensive, everybody in the family can find something they like, and they are open from six a.m. to ten p.m. This little grill is a local hangout for everybody from five to ninety-five years old. They've found their niche and they're succeeding at it.

Not a block away is a restaurant. This restaurant has undergone remodels, ownership changes, new menu, different styles of food, outdoor seating, crafts for sale, appealing to the teenagers, appealing to the old people—you name it, they've tried it. Nine months out of the year, this restaurant is shut down for remodels or upgrades. The restaurant is expensive, in our experience not very tasty, and is failing miserably.

How in the world does this apply to writing?

Find your niche and focus on what works. Don't make your niche too narrow, but find it. Keep up with market trends as well as you can but don't drastically remake yourself and chase every squirrel, don't overprice your product, and don't worry if you get called a greasy gas station diner.

If you consistently deliver a great product at a reasonable price, I believe you will be successful. I can't promise that, but it makes sense to me.

Be the Sinclair. Isn't that something to aspire to?

Chapter Nine

BEST WRITING TIPS I'VE RECEIVED

Time for some inspiring quotes and advice I've received and used to grow my career and myself over the years.

Work your rear off and never, ever give up.

Do what you're passionate about. Writing is tough. If you love it and you absolutely must write, then write. If you don't love it, you'll be miserable trying to succeed at it. If you love it, you'll have the best job in the world.

Write the next book.

I used to hate this advice, and newbie authors tell me they still hate it. But it's so true. If you get caught up on trying to milk the revenue out of one standalone book, or even one series, it will be tough. It's happened. You've seen one-hit wonders—we all have—but the authors who consistently produce are usually the success stories. Especially in the indie world.

On that subject, I've been asked if newbie authors should throw away their first few books because they're still learning and will lose readers because their first book isn't the quality readers are looking for.

Honest truth? I wish I would have thrown my first few books away, but if anybody would have told me that back in the day, no way would I have listened. Now when fans tell me they've only read one of my first few books, I smile my thanks and cringe inside, wishing they'd picked up a newer book.

I think the truth of the matter is that first drafts are kind of like first books—yes, it is highly unlikely they are your best work. That's okay. It's how we learn and improve, and you have to start somewhere. At least you have words down on the page and having something to work with and improve on, whether that be the first draft of your current WIP, or the first book you've ever written.

On that note, a newer author asked me if he should have a series ready before he launched so he could consistently produce books and a reader wouldn't get frustrated that nothing more was coming. I think it's a fabulous idea. Also, if you wrote even a three-book series to start out, traded critiques or (if you can afford it) paid some great editors to go through book one while you wrote books two and three, and then went back and reworked the first book before you sent it off to copy edits and uploaded, think what you would've learned and improved and how much better your first book launch will be than mine was.

I wish I had known about having a series ready or that first books are crap, but it probably wouldn't have mattered. I thought my first books were brilliant and had no clue how those agents and publishers could reject such masterpieces. I also believe in Peter Pan and the Tooth Fairy. Just ask my husband.

Milk before meat.

A few years ago, I was part of an author conference with

some fabulous authors where we taught newer authors how to become a six-figure author. It was a lot of fun and I loved everyone I met. As I was driving home from the conference, I got sick to my stomach and it hit me that we had given the participants "meat before milk."

What I mean by that is if someone had given me the tools when I was a new author to reach a large audience and maybe even make six figures early on in my career, it would have completely backfired on me. I've already admitted that my first books are not my best work, that I made a lot of mistakes and have improved as a storyteller and a businesswoman. If I had gotten my first books out to a wide audience, I would've probably lost a lot of readers and I wouldn't have had the skills to retain them or the time and ability to write quickly and hold their interest.

There is also the fact that the more readers you acquire, the more nasty reviews you'll get. Sadly true. Go look at some big-name authors and I bet they have some ugly reviews. As a newer author, that would've devastated me and I might not have kept going. Now I only look at the five-star reviews. I don't need negativity in my life. If I wanted that, I'd watch the news.

Some authors are a lot more knowledgeable, more with-it than I am, and could be ready to target a large audience with their first books. So take this with a grain of salt, but for me writing is like a lot of things in life. I had to learn a lot to realize what I didn't know, and though I always wanted to get to the goal quickly, I've realized the journey was worth taking and the lessons are ones I'm happy I learned. The lessons have made me who I am.

So if you hit it big quick, that is awesome, but if you're like me and the path is twisted and sometimes steep and covered in rocks and thorns, don't sweat it. Climbing over those rocks makes us stronger, even if we scrape our knee or knuckles on the way. Luckily we heal.

Find a fabulous author group.

I already spent a chapter on this, but honestly it could be the most important thing. You need the resources, talent, support, and love a good group of friends can give you. Writing is a solitary pursuit. Don't end up the hermit and all alone. Give and receive and you'll be blessed for it.

On that subject, I'd be cautious about spending too much time on Facebook groups, email, and online forums. They can each be a time suck, and unless you know those people personally, they might not have your best interests at heart. I've seen some advice on Facebook writing groups that I wouldn't give to my worst enemy. Thankfully, I don't think I have any enemies, but you know what I mean. I firmly believe there is plenty of success for all of us and we should try to build up and help other writers. Sadly, I've seen that not all writers share that theory, so be careful what advice you take and pray hard to know if it's the right advice for you. I know I've already said this, but what works for me might not work for you, for a variety of reasons— timing, personality, family situations, health, writing genre, etc. So yes, learn from other authors, but pray and get your own inspiration to do what works for you.

Don't complain, compare, or criticize.

Negativity and comparisons will only hurt you. Don't waste your time comparing yourself to someone else's ranking on Amazon or their number of newsletter followers. Especially don't waste energy being around people who are Negative Nellies.

Build others up. Love God, love others, and love yourself.

Our family focuses on no complaining, no criticizing, and no negative self-talk. It's crazy sad how many times we put ourselves down. Push those thoughts away and focus on what your Heavenly Father would say to you if you'd only listen. He loves you and He knows your infinite worth and potential. Focus on that.

Growing up, I heard a lot about "mourning with those that mourn." To me, that means being there for those who are going through hard times and trying to ease their burdens. So important. And I believe it's as important to cheer for those who cheer. It's easy to feel bad for and help somebody who's down, but sometimes it's harder to be happy for those who are having success and great times, especially if we want that success ourselves. If you look for the good in other people and hope for their success, it will come around and they'll cheer for you as well.

Side story: All my boys love lacrosse. When my oldest son started playing the sport twelve years ago, it was not well known in our valley and was a club sport even at the high school level. He loved it so much he didn't care and he practiced long hours and worked hard to succeed. He ended up traveling the nation with the Fellowship of Christian Athletes and having incredible experiences, but it was still sometimes depressing for him and his local friends to work so hard and have very few fans or other students come to high school games.

When he and his buddies were juniors and seniors, they became the "super fans" of their school. For every single sport, especially the girls' sports, they would stand in the front row, cheering their friends on. Yes, they were sometimes obnoxious and gave the athletic director and principal a few gray hairs with their cheers, but they kept their language clean and for the most part their cheering was positive.

Fast forward to spring lacrosse season of their senior year. We had untold students and even parents and teachers show up for the varsity lacrosse games. My husband ended up being the emcee and a good friend did the music. Our lacrosse mom threw out prizes and we board members did concessions. It was a party, and Denver had the best senior year imaginable.

I can't tell you how many times I'd be walking the sidelines or stands at a game and ask somebody, "Now who are you here for?"

They'd point at the field and say, "Those boys supported me." Or, "Those boys supported my son, niece, neighbor, friend, or student."

It was cool. It was fun. It was inspiring. Those boys truly cheered for others and it came around in a positive way for them. Do the same with your career. Hope for the good for others. There is enough success for all of us.

One of my author friends read this book draft and asked me to include the following: "You sell yourself short in this book, because as I've already mentioned a couple times, you have always given more than you received. You never once showed up to writing group without your critiques done. You always pay your editor the minute you receive an invoice. You are super generous with newsletter trades, even with baby authors. You are definitely a person who casts her bread upon the waters, not knowing if it will ever come back but willing to help people out regardless."

So right there you see what I mean about the incredible authors I'm able to know and love and support. So grateful.

Sunday.

The Sabbath is truly a day of rest for my family. We go to church, serve others, study the gospel together, and enjoy each other. No cleaning, no writing, no errands, no yard work, no work for me, my honey, or my boys. We cook and bake and invite a lot of people over to eat with us.

This wonderful break makes the rest of my crazy life possible. Every day but Sunday, work as hard as you are capable of.

A few weeks ago, late on a Friday night, I finished an edit and sent it off to one of my editors. My husband asked if I got the book done and I said, "Yes, and I don't have to deal with anything else until Monday."

He looked at me in shock and asked, "A two-day weekend? Who does that?"

We both laughed because neither of us take Saturday off very often. We take a lot of vacations together, and often we even work there, but at least we get away to enjoy each other and our family and friends.

I talked about balance earlier. It's tough. I try every day to put God and my family first. I struggle with it, but I try. I guess that's all we can do is keep trying, right? I know God blesses us for every good effort and intention we have.

Confidence and overcoming insecurities.

I've struggled with confidence my entire life. I wonder if most people don't. It's a tough world we live in and when you put yourself out there, sometimes you get slammed back down. Especially when you put yourself out there on a wider scale. You open yourself up to more criticism and people who don't agree with the way you do things.

I fight my insecurities with knowledge: learning more about my craft and trying to improve my storytelling abilities. And lots and lots of prayer.

It's hard believing that I'm smart enough, imaginative enough, or brave enough to make it in such a tough industry. I'll let you know if I ever overcome my confidence and insecurity issues. I deal well with them, but definitely haven't overcome them.

On that subject, sometimes you have to fake it until you make it. I've walked into writing conferences before with my best outfit on and a smile on my face even as my gut is churning in horror. Sometimes you have to just keep smiling and trying and faking that you are confident and have a handle on everything. Sometimes you can even make yourself believe it.

Confidence in God is key.

Doing what you say you'll do and trusting yourself is also essential.

Don't take yourself or those stupid negative reviews too seriously. Everybody who puts themselves out there will get a nasty review or get made fun of at some point. It's life. My sister would tell me, "Give Satan the bird finger and keep on trucking."

Truly, when someone tries to hurt you, it will only hurt them in the long run. I say a prayer to forgive them for their stupidity and try to shove the negativity from my mind.

On that note, try to surround yourself with positive people. We all get down, especially when things aren't turning out the way we want or somebody makes fun of or attacks us. If you have positive people you can turn to, they will lift and build you up. If I had a dollar for every time I've called or emailed Jennifer Youngblood because I needed her positive attitude, I'd be a billionaire. I should probably be paying her those dollars.

Above all, turn to God. He will never let you down or turn you away. He always has your back.

Dream big and work hard, but don't allow yourself to be distracted from what matters most.

As I'm a natural workaholic (farm girl habits are hard to

break), I have to structure my day so I can get my work done but not miss out on my family, loving God, and loving others. Sometimes I mess it all up, but that's all right. Our Savior lived for us and then suffered and gave His life for us so He could help us pick ourselves up when we fail and try again. He cares about your big problems and your little ones.

"Keep trying. Keep trusting. Keep believing. Keep growing. Heaven will be cheering you on today, tomorrow, and forever." Jeffrey R. Holland

My Guiding Principles:

God

Family

Gratitude

Prayer

Sabbath Day Observance

Service

Work hard. Play hard. Pray hard.

"Get on your knees and pray. And then get on your feet and work." Gordon B. Hinckley

"I must work the works of him that sent me, while it is day: the night cometh, when no man can work. As long as I am in the world, I am the light of the world." John 9:4-5

Blessings for light, love, and success,

Cami

You work with self-imposed deadlines a lot. How do you meet them? What advice would you give to someone who has struggled with this?

For me, if a deadline is on my calendar, it's a promise to myself. I would never break a promise to someone else, so I can't break a promise to myself either.

I also make sure that I schedule my days and weeks so I will stay on target for my deadlines. If you get behind, you can usually restructure and catch up but if you get desperately behind it is sometimes impossible to catch up.

How do you not hit the snooze button every morning?

Ha! I do sometimes, I promise.

I also let myself sleep in on Sunday, so that helps me keep my schedule for the rest of the week. Mostly I don't hit snooze too often because I know how miserable it will be if I fall behind on my day.

You have tough skin. A lot of creatives don't. Is there any advice you

*can give on having tough skin with beta readers, editors, and *gasp**
reviewers?

It is tough! It's a gradual process like anything. I've had reviews and edits that have left me in a funk or ticked me off. I pray for help to forgive and look past it. I also take a break and spend time with my family and that helps restore me. I call my sister and she'll get all defensive and ticked off for me and it seriously helps to have her cussing some unknown reviewer and then I can laugh about it.

Over the years, I've been able to find editors I trust and love to make the book better while not being belittling or degrading. I also try to not even look at bad reviews. Sadly I fail at that too!

Do you actually turn off your email and other internet distractions
for 6 hours a day? Can you shine a brighter light on that? Have you ever
died from disconnecting for that long?

I only disconnect completely if I'm on a vicious deadline. I try to keep the internet turned off on my laptop, which I use to create. Every thousand words written, or every chapter edited, I take a break and then I'll check emails and texts.

Is it important for an author to read? Any advice on picking books to
read?

I think it's essential. I was a reader long before I found my passion for writing. I love books. So many different kinds, but only fiction. Who wants to live in the real world? ;) Because I have Kindle Unlimited, I borrow a lot of different clean and Christian books for free. I make myself give the author twenty pages of my reading time. If they haven't captured my interest by then, I move on. Everybody likes different styles, but I'm a fast-paced girl, so I want action or romance or some kind of hook on page one. It's a fun exercise to help me remember to do the same. Whenever I'm writing or even setting up promotions or newsletters, I think, "What would I want as a reader?" And I try to steer it that way.

Did critiquing other authors along the way help you succeed?

For sure. It's hard to critique and edit and you learn a lot about everything to do with story. It's like the year my oldest son stepped in as the goalie because no one else would. He told me he learned more about the game in that year than the twelve other years of playing lacrosse. Seeing the field from a different view is huge. Even if it stinks to get shot at with a hard ball that leaves huge bruises.

Do you really not watch television?

I don't ever choose to watch television. If I have spare time, I want to be reading. I watch college lacrosse games with my boys and sometimes they'll get me to watch Shark Tank or Grand Tour. I do like movies. Occasionally on a Sunday afternoon, we'll find a movie to watch together. Once or twice a year, I go to the movie theater with my family. I'm always amazed at how great the movie was. My husband always replies, "Yeah, they do a pretty good job." As he shakes his head in bewilderment at me.

How do you deal with those days that don't go according to plan?

Yikes, I hate those days! I love my schedule. I also don't like negativity and when things don't go according to plan, I catch myself getting negative and grumpy. So I start with a prayer, then I shake off the frustration, readjust the schedule for the next few days to catch up, and tell myself tomorrow is another day.

You never said one word about how you multi-task, or do you not?

That's funny, but I really don't. While I run or lift weights in the morning, I listen to inspirational talks by my church leaders. That's probably the only time I multi-task. If I try to multi-task in other areas, I find myself messing something up and having to fix it later.

Do you use beta readers?

I don't. Before I could hire professional editors, I used a lot of critique exchanges and beta readers. They were all great and I really appreciate their time and help, but sometimes they gave conflicting ideas and opinions. I found myself getting distracted and worried by their comments and ended up second-guessing myself a lot.

It was really nice and streamlined my process a lot when I could pay for professional, high-quality editing. I have developed such an incredible rapport and trust with my editors that I know any suggestion they make will make the book better, and that is always my end goal: The best book possible.

What about your review crew?

I think I'm the odd author out here but I don't use a review crew very often. I used to have one and occasionally I'll ask them for a review, but honestly reviews don't seem to sell books and I'd rather have a genuine review than a forced one. Also, from my current understanding Amazon prefers verified reviews, so I'd rather have those if I can. Someday I might use a review crew again. Like I said earlier, the only constant is change, so you have to roll with the changes.

Did you struggle to admit that you were writing a book before you ever published it? And if so, did you have someone close to you read it, or did you keep your writing to yourself?

I was so stoked about my passion for writing that I wanted to share it with everybody. I had some family and friends who were as excited as I was, but I also had some who were cautious, either because they were worried about me being rejected or they just thought I was crazy and didn't have what it took to succeed.

How in the world do you write so many books so quickly? The list of books you have published is really long, and you don't seem anywhere near old enough to have written that many.

Every single day, I sit my bum in the chair. I love to run long distance as well as write. Any runner knows you don't run a marathon without slowly building up your weekly miles and your endurance. As I said in chapter two, it was a process of getting my writing and release speed up. The past couple years I've released two books a month pretty consistently, so that has definitely upped my number of releases.

You release books so quickly during a series. How do you keep all the story plot lines straight and the individual character voices separate from each other?

I have a word doc that lines out the books and series to keep things straight. For me, the characters are definitely their own people, so when I'm focused on and immersed in their story, they come alive in my head. I would not be shocked at all to meet one of them on the street. That'd be cool. I'm waiting for that day.

Thanks for reading! If you have any questions or ideas I'd love to hear them – cami@camichecketts.com.

Hugs and much love,

Cami

ALSO BY CAMI CHECKETTS

Delta Family Romances

Deceived

Abandoned

Committed

Famous Friends Romances

Loving the Firefighter

Loving the Athlete

Loving the Rancher

Loving the Coach

Loving the Contractor

Loving the Sheriff

Loving the Entertainer

The Hidden Kingdom Romances

Royal Secrets

Royal Security

Royal Doctor

Royal Mistake

Royal Courage

Royal Pilot

Royal Imposter

Royal Baby

Royal Battle

Royal Fake Fiancé

Secret Valley Romance

Sister Pact

Marriage Pact

Christmas Pact

Famous Friends Romances

Loving the Firefighter

Loving the Athlete

Loving the Rancher

Loving the Coach

Loving the Sheriff

Loving the Contractor

Loving the Entertainer

Survive the Romance

Romancing the Treasure

Romancing the Escape

Romancing the Boat

Romancing the Mountain

Romancing the Castle

Romancing the Extreme Adventure

Romancing the Island

Romancing the River

Romancing the Spartan Race

Mystical Lake Resort Romance

Only Her Undercover Spy

Only Her Cowboy

Only Her Best Friend

Only Her Blue-Collar Billionaire

Only Her Injured Stuntman

Only Her Amnesiac Fake Fiancé

Only Her Hockey Legend

Only Her Smokejumper Firefighter

Only Her Christmas Miracle

Jewel Family Romance

Do Marry Your Billionaire Boss

Do Trust Your Special Ops Bodyguard

Do Date Your Handsome Rival

Do Rely on Your Protector

Do Kiss the Superstar

Do Tease the Charming Billionaire

Do Claim the Tempting Athlete

Do Depend on Your Keeper

Strong Family Romance

Don't Date Your Brother's Best Friend

Her Loyal Protector

Don't Fall for a Fugitive

Her Hockey Superstar Fake Fiance

Don't Ditch a Detective

Don't Miss the Moment

Don't Love an Army Ranger

Don't Chase a Player

Don't Abandon the Superstar

Steele Family Romance

Her Dream Date Boss

The Stranded Patriot

The Committed Warrior

Extreme Devotion

Quinn Family Romance

The Devoted Groom

The Conflicted Warrior

The Gentle Patriot

The Tough Warrior

Her Too-Perfect Boss

Her Forbidden Bodyguard

Running Romcom

Running for Love

Taken from Love

Saved by Love

Cami's Collections

Hidden Kingdom Romance Collection

Survive the Romance Collection

Mystical Lake Resort Romance Collection

Billionaire Boss Romance Collection

Jewel Family Collection

The Romance Escape Collection

Onboard for Love

Shadows in the Curtain

Billionaire Bride Pact Romance

The Resilient One

The Feisty One

The Independent One

The Protective One

The Faithful One

The Daring One

Park City Firefighter Romance

Rescued by Love

Reluctant Rescue

Stone Cold Sparks

Snowed-In for Christmas

Echo Ridge Romance

Christmas Makeover

Last of the Gentlemen

My Best Man's Wedding

Change of Plans

Counterfeit Date

Snow Valley

Full Court Devotion: Christmas in Snow Valley

A Touch of Love: Summer in Snow Valley

Running from the Cowboy: Spring in Snow Valley

Light in Your Eyes: Winter in Snow Valley

Romancing the Singer: Return to Snow Valley

Fighting for Love: Return to Snow Valley

Other Books by Cami

Seeking Mr. Debonair: Jane Austen Pact

Seeking Mr. Dependable: Jane Austen Pact

Saving Sycamore Bay

Oh, Come On, Be Faithful

Protect This

Blog This

Redeem This

The Broken Path

Dead Running

Dying to Run

Fourth of July

Love & Loss

Love & Lies

ABOUT THE AUTHOR

Cami is a part-time author, part-time exercise consultant, part-time housekeeper, full-time wife, and overtime mother of four adorable boys. Sleep and relaxation are fond memories. She's never been happier.

Join Cami's VIP list to find out about special deals, giveaways and new releases and receive a free copy of *Seeking Mr. Debonair: The Jane Austen Pact* by clicking here.

Keep reading for an excerpt of Cami's latest clean romantic adventure: *Loving the Entertainer*.

cami@camichecketts.com
www.camichecketts.com

Sawyer Creed jogged down the pine-needle covered trail as a light rain fell around him. The Oregon mountains on a May day were beautiful, but he could only focus on one beauty. The one who was walking quickly away from him, holding her daughter's hand. Kate Elisabet, thankfully not Lanza any longer. The love of his life. She'd ditched him harshly and thoroughly enough at eighteen that he'd thought he'd learned his lesson. He'd avoided her for ten long years, mostly because he couldn't stand to see her with her loser husband and know she'd chosen the scum of all scums Richard Lanza over him.

But no, he had learned nothing. A couple minutes in Kate's glorious presence and he was a smitten idiot all over again. He'd also avoided getting close to her for the past ten years for his own sanity. The moment she fixed those blue eyes on him, all the memories of their happy, carefree time together and how much he had loved her hit him like a freight train. He still loved her and was a glutton for more punishment at her lovely hands.

Her daughter looked over her shoulder and her beautiful face brightened. She looked like a carbon copy of her mother. Thankfully, she looked nothing like her weasel of a father. He'd questioned over and over again how Kate could've cheated on him with the likes of Richard Lanza, but Carmen was proof it had happened. Sawyer would've forgiven her and married her in an instant, but she hadn't given him that chance. Apparently Richard was "steady and good and trustworthy."

He knew Kate had learned better than anybody that those descriptors were far from the truth. Richard had abused her, belittled her, controlled her, and cheated on her. It didn't give Sawyer any satisfaction that she had learned the truth about her husband, only a sick sadness for what she'd gone through.

"Mama," Carmen said. "It's Mr. Creed."

The little girl was adorable. It was insane that she was Richard Lanza's daughter. The snake should not have been blessed with a wife like Kate and a daughter like Carmen, but that was life. The only good news was Richard had been arrested last fall, over six months ago now. He'd skipped bail and his whereabouts were unknown. From Sawyer's inside source, Jake, he'd learned Kate had recently been awarded a divorce. Knowing she was finally single again was one reason Sawyer had come home to visit, even if he hadn't admitted it to anyone but himself.

Was it finally his and Kate's time? Their beautiful valley set on the southern Oregon coast was free of the Lanza men. Phillip and Jonathon were dead and Richard had run off like the skunk he was.

Most of the credit for Phillip, Richard, and Jonathon being taken to task was thanks to Sawyer's group of incredible friends, the Flyers. Sawyer loved his friends and would do anything for them. From eighteen to twenty-eight, he'd had three missions in life—avoid Kate at all costs, make his friends and himself famous, and prove to his mother and himself that he was not "a pathetic waste of space and a failure just like your father." That was a direct quote he'd heard far too often growing up.

He'd accomplished everything except making Jake famous. Jake had reiterated over and over again that he didn't want to be famous. His friend kept alluding his attempts and Sawyer loved Jake enough to let it go. He could humble himself and change his mission statement.

Today, he would rewrite it to include two tasks. Focus number one: let go of the anger over Kate cheating on him with Richard and ditching him, and focus number two: get Kate to fall for him again.

She spun around to glare at him. He slowed his steps so he wouldn't run them over and realized his second focus might be tougher than he'd thought.

"Hey." He put on his cheerful grin. It had been touted as "charismatic, irresistible, enigmatic, sexy" by fans, media, and influencers alike. No woman could resist his grin, or so he was told.

Carmen returned his smile, but Kate's face tightened. No beautiful, welcoming smile appeared.

He spread his hands—innocently, he hoped.

Kate's gaze traveled over his upper body and her cheeks turned pink. She focused on a tree. Hopefully, that appreciative look in her gorgeous blue eyes boded well for him. He was incredibly fit, and he had yet to meet a woman who didn't admire his handsome face and impressive physique. Wooing them with his charming personality was easier than throwing a backflip on downhill skis. Wooing Kate might be more the level of triple backflip. Sadly he hadn't perfected one yet and the crashes stung almost as much as Kate not smiling at him.

Kate had hurt him worse than any physical pain from failing at a stunt or getting injured. She was his weakness, his love, and the only woman who'd ever dumped him. His confidence around her was lower than if someone had shoved him back into his childhood home.

He pushed those memories away. He'd keep his smile and fake it until he made it. No one would know how uncertain he was of his reception with her and his hopes for their future.

"Can I walk you to your car?" he asked.

"We're fine," Kate insisted. She turned and strode off down the trail. That flick of her long, blond hair over her shoulder was so familiar, but missing now was the memory of her sweet, accepting smile.

Carmen jogged to keep up, but waved at him over her shoulder. At least her daughter seemed to like him. From what his friends had said, that was a big deal. Carmen and Kate had been abused and belittled for far too long. The little girl was reluctant and afraid around most men. She'd warmed up to Jake and Jared so far. Sawyer understood belittlement from a parent. It was difficult to move past. Even as an adult. He wanted to be the one to help the adorable girl.

He'd gathered information on these two while trying to act like he wasn't interested. Kate breaking his heart at eighteen and choosing Richard over him, then finding out she'd cheated on him while he thought she loved him, had been as big of a motivator to be ultra-successful and do crazy stunts as proving his mom wrong. He'd dated many women around the world, but he'd never found Kate's equal.

Kate was now available, so he'd planned to assess the situation, see how she and her daughter were doing emotionally, and see how Kate reacted to him. If need be, he'd been certain he was mature enough and had enough life experiences that he could stay strong and aloof when he saw her again. He should've known better. One look in those blue eyes and all plans flew out the window. His heart was a goner.

He hadn't become an international influencer and social media superstar by standing around and waiting for something good to happen. He worked hard and he chased after the dream. The dream was Kate Elisabet. It always had been, even if he'd denied that truth for ten long years. Luckily, those years had been extremely busy and had gone fast despite how much he'd longed for her. He was confident now, hardly ever heard his mother's snarky voice in his head, and refused to accept rejection or failure. He wasn't about to take either right now.

He broke into a jog again and easily caught them. Walking casually next to Carmen, he smiled at her, not letting himself look at Kate. Carmen smiled back.

"I think I'd better escort you to your car. There's a fierce animal in these woods and I wouldn't want beautiful ladies like the two of you at risk from such a creature."

Kate sucked in a breath. He didn't let himself look at her. Yet. But she had to remember. He'd used this ploy to get her alone and kiss her the first time.

It had taken him several years to get Kate to notice him and fall for him. The summer before their senior year, they'd been at a church youth activity, a fire in the woods not far from here. He'd told her this same story, made her laugh, and she'd agreed to a short walk in the dark woods where, of course, he'd protect her from the "fierce animal."

He'd never forget that night. The smell of wood smoke

competing with her soft peach scent, the fire she'd revealed for him in her kiss, and the softness of her in his arms. He still didn't understand how the fire of their love had been doused. He had to figure out how to rekindle it.

"Animal?" Carmen's eyes widened, and she looked around quickly.

"Not to worry," Sawyer reassured her. "I'm here to protect you." He poked out his chest and flexed his right arm. Carmen giggled, but he could tell she was still nervous. "This animal is terrified of me, so I'll keep you safe."

He finally let himself look at Kate's gorgeous face. She had an ethereal quality about her, so beautiful it almost made a man wonder if she was truly part angel or maybe a mystical creature.

He'd stayed strong and not pursued her for ten long years simply by staying away. Now, five minutes in her presence and he was acting like a fool.

At the moment, she was giving him an interesting look. It was full of longing, and trepidation. He'd probably have to work harder to win her heart as an adult than he had as a teenager.

To have Kate by his side, it would be worth any sacrifice, time spent, or patience he rarely had to exhibit.

He winked at her and continued with his story, hoping this wouldn't backfire on him and scare Carmen instead of winning her over. It had worked on Kate years ago. He prayed it would work now to help her remember how fun, exciting, and sweet those ten months together during their senior year had been.

"Do you want to know what this fierce animal is so you can spot and avoid them in the future, even if I'm not here to protect you?" Sawyer asked Carmen.

"Yes, please."

The sweet innocence in her blue eyes made him want to truly

protect this little girl. Not just from every animal in the forest, but from any person who would do her harm, most importantly her own father.

"This animal's name ..." he drew out the suspense, making sure he had Carmen's complete attention. He wasn't sure about Kate. She was focused on the trail and didn't look at him. Was she remembering the last time she'd heard this story? Maybe dwelling on all the passionate kisses they'd shared? The kisses that had blown all her defenses away and had her declaring she loved him? She obviously didn't love him any longer, but at least she hadn't sent him away.

He lowered his voice to a stage whisper, "The western gray flying squirrel." He gave them a dramatic nod.

Kate almost laughed, even though she'd known the punch line. She seemed to catch herself and pressed her lips together, focusing again on the thick pine trees surrounding them.

"A squirrel?" Carmen squinted up at him, as if uncertain whether he was pulling her leg.

He kept a serious face. "Yes, ma'am. But not just any squirrel. A western gray flying squirrel. Fearsome. That squirrel could soar out of those trees at any minute."

Her eyes widened.

Sawyer sprang forward, flipping and twisting his body as if he were doing a sideways flip on a wakeboard. He landed in front of the women and spread his hands wide. "And just like that, no squirrel can get through to you."

Carmen jumped and then giggled, putting a hand over her mouth.

Kate stopped walking and studied him standing in front of them on the trail. She rolled her eyes, but he could see she was fighting a smile. He could also tell that she remembered. His body felt warm all over. They could go back to Jared's house and have dinner with his friends. They'd tuck Carmen into bed with funny stories, songs about Jesus, and a prayer. And then ... he'd take her on a walk down to the ocean and kiss her like she hadn't been kissed in ten years. He knew her loser ex-husband probably kissed like the disgusting snake he was, all lipless and scaly, doing weird things with his tongue.

"And lucky for you," Sawyer continued, making sure the story finished nicely. "I'd be here to flip in front of you and protect you from that vicious creature at a moment's notice."

"Lucky us," Kate said.

Sawyer looked her over and nodded. "Lucky, lucky you." His voice came out far too husky.

Her cheeks tinged pink and her pulse was visibly racing in her neck. Sawyer should congratulate himself—he'd finally seemed to affect her—but he was too busy staring into those blue eyes of hers to waste time gloating, even to himself.

"Mama." Carmen tugged on her mother's hand, breaking their concentration on each other.

"Yes, love?" Kate bent closer to her child.

"He's teasing, right? There's no western gray flying squirrel?"

"Yes, love, he's teasing. He's always teasing."

Sawyer wasn't sure if that was a shot or a compliment. She used to love his teasing. Until she hadn't.

Carmen peered up at him. "You're a funny guy," she said. "I like you."

Score one for Team Creed. "Well, thank you, beautiful lady. I like you too."

Carmen giggled happily. It was a pure, sweet sound.

Kate peered up at Sawyer, and they exchanged the most incredible look. It seemed his Kate was remembering what had happened after he made up the squirrel story the first time. She'd laughed and then she'd bitten her lip. He'd told her if she kept biting her lip, he wouldn't be able to resist kissing her. She hadn't stopped.

And then he'd held heaven in his arms.

The memories of that first incredible kiss hadn't dimmed for him. Had they for her? She might simply appreciate him making Carmen laugh. From what he understood, there hadn't been nearly enough laughter in this little girl's life.

They all started walking again. Carmen and Kate held hands and Sawyer walked on the opposite side of Carmen.

The rain had slowed, and it smelled and looked glorious in the thick forest, green and fresh and like the most beautiful May day of his life. He risked a glance at Kate over Carmen's head. She was looking at him, but as soon as their gazes met, she turned quickly and focused on the muddy path. But she had been looking at him. It was something. This entire walk was something. Something huge. For the first time he could remember, he wasn't recording his tricks or playing for a large crowd. He wasn't scheming how to increase his followers, likes, and comments. He'd spent his adult years making himself and his friends famous, all except Jake. He'd just committed to give up on the sheriff's opportunity for fame. It was strangely liberating to have a different focus. He was playing for a crowd of two, but no audience had ever been this important to him.

"Mama, do you think Jake is gonna marry Auntie Alisa?"

"Yes, sweetie. He was proposing to her today. Remember?"

Carmen nodded. She looked up at Sawyer. "Is Jake your friend?"

"Yes, he is."

"He's nice."

Sawyer would never describe the intense, tough yet funny Sheriff Jake Tarbet as "nice," but Jake was a great man, and he imagined all his friends would be extra nice to Carmen. "Yes, he is," he agreed. "Jake is one of the best men I know."

She peered up at him. "Good. If he's marrying my auntie, he'd better be the best."

"For sure." Sawyer had reservations about Alisa simply because she'd been born into the Lanza family, but the woman was a brave sweetheart, and head over heels in love with his friend. She couldn't help who her family was. Sawyer should know and understand that better than anyone. His own mom was a grumpy harpy, and his dad had been a wimpy victim his mom belittled more than she did Sawyer.

"Are you one of the best men you know?" Carmen asked, surprising him out of his bitter thoughts about his parents.

"Well, um ..." How could he answer that without coming across as too cocky or too humble?

Rich laughter spilled out of Kate.

Sawyer stumbled and quickly righted himself. He thought he'd remembered her laugh, but the memories didn't do it justice. Her laugh was beautiful and rich and so Kate. His heart beat quicker.

"She got you," Kate teased. "You can't claim you are the best man because you'll look cocky, but you're not humble enough to say you're not." She grinned at him and he was thrust ten years into the past. That grin was the stuff men went to war over. Richard was gone, so Sawyer hadn't gotten the chance to go to war and avenge her, but he would get to celebrate the victory with the perfect woman. He would sweep her off her feet, spin her around, and then kiss that teasing smile right off her face.

"You're not the best man?" Carmen asked, horror evident in her wide blue gaze.

Kate's laughter was gone so quick Sawyer almost wondered if he'd imagined it. Her face was completely serious. She stopped and bent to Carmen's level. "Sawyer is a good man," she reassured. "A great man. He's one of Jake's friends and he would never, ever hurt us."

Sawyer's heart seemed to fall to his feet. He stared between mother and daughter, and his stomach churned. Richard had disappeared in November and his father Phillip had been killed in March. Sawyer had been around briefly after Kate, Carmen, and Alisa got their freedom from the Lanza tyrants, but he'd headed back on tour not long after. He'd heard that Kate and Carmen had been abused and it had made him furious and sick, but to see the fear in that little girl's eyes and to hear the seriousness in Kate's tone ...

Oh, man. He wasn't sure if he was about to throw up from the nauseated feeling in his gut or storm off, find Richard Lanza, tear the man apart with his bare hands, then come back and assure Carmen that nobody would ever hurt her or her mom. Nobody.

His silly tease with the squirrel and protecting them should've fallen flatter than it did. Kate was not an innocent teenager any longer and Carmen had trust issues larger than Sawyer's fake ego. For some reason, Carmen had laughed and seemed to like him. Could he show the child that many men were good and kind and would protect, respect, and love the women and children in their life, not control, use, or abuse them?

Did he even have the right to protect them? He didn't know, and maybe it was too soon. He'd have to ask Jake's therapist mom how long it would take for someone like Kate to heal. When would Kate be ready for a relationship? Richard had been arrested and then skipped bail and disappeared six months ago, but Phillip had only been killed two months ago. From what Sawyer understood, even after Richard was gone, Phillip had controlled Kate and Alisa and probably terrified Carmen with his constant unstated threats. Alisa seemed to be doing amazing, but she had Jake. Did Kate and Carmen need Sawyer, or did they need time to heal? Was he even the right fit for women who had been through what they had? He wasn't the sensitive type. He was the show-off, the attention-grabber, the charmer, the fun one. Did they need somebody like him?

No woman needs someone like you. It was his mom's voice. He hated it when she crept into his thoughts.

"Okay." Carmen accepted her mom's answer as if it were gospel truth. "I'm glad you're a great man, Sawyer Creed."

Sawyer managed a smile, hoping his emotions weren't showing on his face. "Thank you." He glanced at Kate and the worried look on her face said his emotions were too strong and either she was worried about him upsetting her daughter or worried about him caring for them both too much.

Carmen extended her hand to Sawyer. Kate's eyes widened and then filled with a warmth that lit him up from the inside out. He would do everything in his power to help, love, and earn this woman's trust, and that of her daughter.

Dang. He was a goner, and all Kate had done was say he was a great man and give him a laugh and a soft look. He'd known it would be like this if he were ever in Kate's presence again. He'd fall like the smitten teenager again. But who cared? This was Kate. His Kate. There had to be some deep, dark, awful reason she'd cheated on Sawyer and chosen Richard over him all those years ago. He'd often wondered if the loser had threatened, blackmailed, or tricked her. Now that loser was gone. Could it be their time?

Sawyer wrapped his much larger hand around Carmen's soft, delicate fingers.

Carmen smiled up at him and then the three of them started walking forward. Sawyer was having the strangest, warmest, most incredible feelings stir in him. This little girl. She could have complete power over his heart, just like her mother did, but in a very different way.

"1, 2, 3!" Carmen suddenly cried out.

Kate swung Carmen up, but without Sawyer responding, it was a lame, lopsided swing.

"You're supposed to swing me," Carmen said softly. "Auntie and Mama do it. But you don't have to if you don't want to."

"Oh! I was being a lamebrain." He grinned at her, but even her uncertainty about being too bold to ask him to swing her had him upset about the way she'd been treated. "Let's try again."

Her shy smile came, and she nodded. "Okay. 1, 2, 3!"

They swung at the same time. Carmen's little feet went flying, and she laughed happily.

When her feet returned to the ground, she begged, "Again?"

"For sure. Higher this time," Sawyer said.

"Yay! 1, 2, 3!"

Sawyer quickly transferred her hand to his left hand, put his right hand under her lower back, and swung her almost over his head.

Carmen gave a cry of surprise and then a loud, delighted laugh.

Sawyer gently set her back on her feet. She looked up at him, her blue eyes sparkling like her mom's used to do when he'd pick her up and spin her around before lowering her and kissing her. Did Kate still smell like peaches and taste even sweeter? Did he dare call her the nickname "peaches" again? How soon could he try spinning Kate and then kissing her?

He met her gaze over Carmen's head. Kate blinked at him, bit her lip, and then looked away. The biting at her lip made his blood run hot. It was a habit of hers, but it had become their signal that she wanted him to kiss her. Did that mean she wanted him to kiss her now? A guy could hope.

"That was fun!" Carmen interrupted his longing for her mom's lips.

Sawyer often felt like he was on top of the world, literally with the heights of some of their stunts, but figuratively as he was beloved and followed and liked by so many people. But seeing the delight in this little girl's eyes was an acclaim he'd never sought. It was more rewarding than any review dripping with praise or any crowd chanting his and Corbin's names.

"Again?" he asked.

"Yes, please!"

He met Kate's gaze over the little girl's head several times as Carmen counted and they swung her together. He lifted her higher several times and a couple times he took her from her mom's arms and did a little flip with her slight frame. She was so little it was easy to lift and flip her.

Kate seemed to appreciate the joy he brought to her daughter. Was she ready to appreciate him? Ah, man, he prayed it was their time. Ten years was a long time to ache for the woman he loved.

They cleared the forest and Kate said, "Okay, love. Let's go get in the car."

They walked across the parking lot and around some trees. Sawyer's mind scrambled for something to say. He had to extend their time together. In a few weeks, he'd be heading ... he couldn't remember where. He, Corbin, and Sienna were all over the map, but mostly in tropical locations. He loved what they did, but would he ever settle down and have a family? As he looked at Kate and Carmen and they gave him identical sweet smiles, his heart thumped faster. He didn't have any desire to settle down, but a family sounded amazing. Could he talk Kate into traveling with him? Carmen could homeschool. The experiences he could give these two would only enrich her education and their lives.

He opened the back door of the older Mazda for Carmen and she slid in, reaching up with her fist. "Knuckles," she cried out.

He bumped her knuckles and grinned. "Thanks for letting me protect you from the squirrels."

She giggled. "Thanks for swinging me so high!"

"Anytime." He waved and gently shut her door, turning to her exquisite mother. "Hey," he said softly.

Kate looked him over and then reached for her door handle. Sawyer put his hand over hers. Warmth filled him at the simple touch. Kate glanced sharply up at him. He swallowed and eased closer. He thought he had Carmen's vote. Could he get Kate's?

He tried to think what to say. Something suave and appealing. Something to convince her to give him a chance after all this time.

"Hey," he managed again.

Come on, Creed, you're a rock star with women and conversation. He'd had easy conversations with the future queen of Magna and female diplomats and movie stars, but Kate tied his tongue. The pressure to get this right was huge.

He put one hand on the top of her beat-up car and leaned closer, giving her his patented smoldering look. Words weren't usually necessary when he used that look.

"I am *not* doing this with you," she said, far too sharp, and obviously not falling for him.

He eased back, stunned, and said very eloquently, "Oh."

Her blue eyes snapped at him. What had he done wrong and where were all the warm, sweet looks from when they'd walked down the path and swung Carmen between them? Why had she done the sexy lip-biting thing if she didn't want him?

"I appreciate you being cute with Carmen," Kate continued. "She obviously loved that. But I'm *not* one of your women, Sawyer. I have to protect Carmen at all costs, and you flitting in and out of her life would be horrible for her. Worse would be watching you get killed during one of your stunts."

His eyes widened. She'd read his desire for her and knew exactly what his intentions were. He wanted her, just as he always had. Her response was interesting. It wasn't that he wasn't good enough for her as he'd always feared, but she'd watched him date different women over the years and she needed stability for Carmen.

It all made sense. But it also frustrated him. First, he couldn't commit to settling down in Emerald Coast and he would not stop doing his stunts. She had him there. Second, he was the one who got dumped, cheated on, and crapped on ten years ago. He should demand an explanation and she should apologize and work to get back into his good graces, not the other way around. He had no problem humbling himself for her, if she'd at least meet him ten percent of the way.

"Carmen's a doll," he said, to give himself some time to think this through.

"Thank you."

He waited, but she gave him nothing; no lingering look, no sweet smile. His pride got the best of him, and he lifted his hands. "Hey, it's no skin off my back if you don't want to be one of my women," he said, hating himself. One of his women? She was *the* one.

Her eyes narrowed. "It's ridiculous how they crawl all over you, and no, I don't want to be one of your women."

It stung. No, it burned deep. She didn't want him. He wasn't enough for the beautiful Kate Elisabet. Why was he surprised? His mom would've told him as much, if he'd ever asked.

He scrambled to save face and folded his arms across his chest. "As you obviously have noticed, Googling me constantly over the last ten years, I've got plenty of women chasing me, tracking me down, just hoping for a chance with me." He gave her a cocky smirk when he wanted to drop to the ground and beg her to give him a chance. He'd chase her. He'd do anything. He could make more regular visits to Emerald Coast. He could be more cautious with his stunts. She and Carmen could travel with him.

No other woman compared to Kate. Never had. Never would. Not for him.

Her eyes traveled over his upper body, then met his gaze again. Her lips tightened. "Glad we got that clear."

She yanked the door open, slid inside, and slammed it shut.

Sawyer wanted to bang on the window, rip the door open, tell her his last few sentences had been stupid lies born of even stupider pride. He wanted to explain to her exactly how much he still loved her.

Instead, he stayed in his role, impressive for him as he knew he wore his emotions too openly. He stepped back and lifted a hand, keeping the smirk on his face and the desire for her out of his eyes. She only looked at him once, then quickly away.

Carmen waved as they backed out. He waved back.

Within seconds, they were gone. The smile left Sawyer's face, and all hope left his heart. One simple walk with his dream woman. That was all he'd get.

Where was Corbin? He needed to risk his life and then he'd go find some woman to take to the dinner Jared and Eve were hosting for the Flyers and their wives. There were always plenty of women waiting around, hoping to get noticed by him.

Sadly, he knew no stunt or beautiful date would heal the ache in his heart. Nothing but Kate could heal him. And she didn't want him.

———

Keep reading here.

www.ingramcontent.com/pod-product-compliance
Lightning Source LLC
Chambersburg PA
CBHW050038260726

48658CB00005B/1673